THIS BOOK IS PUBLISHED BY INGRID CLAUS

Illustrations are designed by Judith A. Gavin-Holton
and, in part, by Valerie Houser

Library of Congress Cataloging-in-Publication Data available upon request.
ISBN-13: 978-1477426289
ISBN-10: 1477426280

Printed in the United States of America

May 2012

Dedication:

To my precious granddaughter, Kailyn, and her loving and caring Mom Karin, who I love with all my heart.

Acknowledgments:

A special thank you goes to my husband, companion, and friend Bryan, who inspired and encouraged me to write about our EIGHTY in the first place. Many, many thanks to Mary D. Scott for her indispensable computer help in the creation of this book. I could have never done it without her.

Author's note:

This book is based on a true story. Eighty was part of our family for almost nineteen wonderful years. She was a very special addition to our family and will live forever in our hearts.

Enjoy my story.

- Ingrid Claus

The Little Black Traveling Cat:

EIGHTY

Volume Two

THE RED-EYED DEER & THE STINKY SKUNK

BY

INGRID CLAUS

Illustrations by Judith A. Gavin-Holton
and, in part, by Valerie Houser

HELLO, MY NAME IS EIGHTY.

Spring was finally here. It was time to hook up our Super-Cool-Travel-Trailer.

Mom had put Puppy in the car. Then she carried Oreo to her seat. What was up with that? Mom always put me in the car before Oreo. I did not know what to make of it. Did that mean I had to stay home alone? Oh no, I did not even want to think about *that*. I had to act quickly and get mom's attention before they drove off. I arched my back and cried as loud as I could: "Mom (MEOW, Mom (MEOW), wait for *me*. Don't leave me." When mom came running, I stopped calling. She asked me why I was so upset. Didn't she know why? After all she was my mother and should know why. When I stared at her with my beautiful green eyes she figured it out. "We would never leave you behind, Eighty," she said. That was exactly what I needed to hear. I brushed up against her legs practically dancing around her while *purrrring* for joy. My way of letting mom know that I was a happy little cat again. She picked me up to join the rest of the family.

It felt good to be back on the open road. The windows were slightly rolled down. We were breathing in clean, fresh air, and could feel the wind brush our fur. Our older and wiser friend, Oreo, told Puppy and I about mountains, waterfalls, forests, lakes, and beautiful wild flowers in vibrant and pastel colors growing everywhere. She pointed out big and small wild animals, birds, bees, and butterflies. She explained to us how magical Mother Nature is with her four seasons. Do *you* know what they are? Well, let me tell you. They are called spring, summer, fall, and winter. Oreo always said that each season has its own beauty. She especially liked it when colorful rainbows appeared in the sky. She would say to Puppy and I: "Look at that beautiful rainbow, you two. Close your eyes and make a wish. After making your wish you can open your eyes again. Some day your wish may come true."

It was early evening when we finally arrived at our destination.

We were very tired from the long trip and decided to get a good night's

rest. Rain started falling and splashing against the windows. Perfect time to

cuddle up next to each other and have the sound of the rain *sing*

us to sleep.

The bright sun and singing birds woke us early the next morning.

I jumped up and looked out the window, and what did I see? Squirrels were

rubbing their eyes with their tiny front paws. Gophers and ground squirrels

were peeking out of their homes to see if any hawks were circling above. I

watched rabbits with their big ears, their twitching noses, and their stubby,

fluffy little tails hop from bush to bush.

The soil had not dried out from the overnight rain. The ground was

soggy and mushy, but mom took Puppy for a walk right after breakfast

anyway. Oreo was doing her stretching exercises on her bed, when it was

my turn to go and seek adventure.

I loved the feel of the cold, wet, squishy soil between my toes. Once

in a while a wet leaf would get stuck to the bottom of my paw.

So I stopped, lifted up my leg and had mom remove the leaf. When we got to the forest she picked me up and put me on her shoulder. I liked sitting up there. The view was great.

All of a sudden mom stopped in her tracks. She pulled tightly on my leash, grabbed me, and tucked me under her arm. But why, I thought **purrrring** with delight. Wow, did I get a big surprise. I did not believe my eyes. A tall gray animal with fiery- red- eyes was glaring right at us. It could not have been more than ten feet away. Where did that **beast** come from? Mom squeezed me tightly while she was whispering to me: "Eighty, be very, very still and do not make any kind of noise so we don't spook the deer." **That** huge thing was a deer? I had seen many deer before but none of them were that big. The deer's red eyes were wide open and totally fixated on us. It was chewing on something. The jaws and big lips were moving nervously up and down and sideways. Saliva was running out of both corners of its mouth dropping to the forest floor. The deer was stomping on the ground with its right hoof over and over again.

I could feel mom trembling with fear. All I could do was listen and wonder what was going to happen next. We did not want to frighten the deer. We were no match for that wild **beast**. Hopefully, it would calm down and realize that we did not want to harm it. Mom had no idea what to do. Was that big animal thinking of attacking us? It was certainly powerful enough.

It seemed we were standing there for hours when actually only minutes had gone by. Without saying anything, mom started backing up very, very slowly, step by step. She was keeping an eye on the deer to make sure it was not charging toward us. All of a sudden the deer appeared to be totally calm. It was just standing there. It looked away from us and with lightning speed disappeared into the dense forest. Mom put me back up on her shoulder. She was still very much shaken. I started **purrrring.** That made her feel better and calmed her nerves. Mom said: "Eighty, we got very lucky that the deer did not attack us. I don't know what was wrong with it, but it looked sick. Let's get out of here before it decides to return."

We turned away from the pine trees and all the little critters who roamed the forest floor. I kept my eyes wide open looking around to see if I would spot something else that might not want us in their territory.

Without further incident we arrived at our camping spot. I tried to tell Dad, Puppy, and Oreo in my high pitched voice about our adventure. They could not understand me, so I let mom do all the talking. After she was finished telling her story, she praised me for listening and keeping very still. She petted me on top of my head and under my chin. She even gave me one potato chip as a reward and it was very *Yummy*.

Dad told mom that it was too dangerous to take me walking in those woods by herself. Not another human soul had been around. If the deer had attacked us, there would have been no one to come to our rescue. It could have ended in tragedy. Oreo and Puppy were listening intensely about our adventure and did not like thinking about all the danger our mom and I had been in.

NEWS

It had been an exciting but frightening day. I was exhausted and went to bed but could not fall asleep. I kept seeing the fiery- red-eyed deer. Puppy and Oreo could sense that I was a little nervous about closing my eyes and falling asleep. Both of my companions came over and curled up to me, one on each side. They wanted me to know that they were there for me in case I had a bad dream about the giant *red-eyed beast*. My old, wise friend *purrrred* until I went to sleep.

Oreo and Puppy did not really know how much I appreciated their friendship and protection. I could always count on their help if I had a problem.

When I woke up the next morning my friends were still by my side. I rushed to look out the window. I was very disappointed when I saw raindrops all over the window. It was still raining. What would my two friends and I do all day without being able to explore the surroundings?

I spotted a big log lying in the bushes. Wow, it would be so much fun to go and investigate. Was it possible that part of the log was hollow? That would be totally awesome. I could crawl inside and look for bugs, grubs, beetles, and other little critters. I remembered how tasty they were. When I was younger I used to catch them and eat them. Mom did not like that at all. Neither did Oreo. One time when I had tasted a few she swatted me with her paw. I got the message right away that she did not want me to pick them up and eat them.

Midmorning the sun started peeking through the clouds. It was time to get some exercise. Mom did not want us roaming through the wet bushes and get all muddy. Puppy was delighted to finally go for a walk.

When mom hooked me up to my red leash, I was all excited and started to run. We came upon a herd of deer. Mom and I compared the size of the red-eyed deer to this herd. Each one of those animals looked so small and graceful. They were grazing very calmly and quietly across a lush green meadow, lifting up their heads once in a while checking out their surroundings. After they had finished eating they all sprinted away one by one vanishing into the forest.

Mom and I strolled back to dad and my two friends who were waiting for us inside the trailer. Before bedding down for the night, we all sat outside for awhile enjoying a campfire and gazing at the moon and the stars.

The sun had just peeked above the horizon the next morning when I was awakened by the aroma of freshly brewed coffee. I know how mom enjoys her first cup of coffee outside while it is still peaceful and quiet. Sometimes I sleep in, but I would rather join her in the fresh air and scope out the area around us. She fastened my collar and leash and tied me to the picnic bench right in front of the camper. "Eighty stay here. I will be right back. I am just getting my coffee." Mom had just gone inside when I saw something stir in the bushes not too far from me. Being a curious cat, I had to check it out. I spotted something with black fur and a white stripe on its back. What could that be? I had never seen anything like it before in my life. I needed to get a little closer to take a good look at this newcomer. This animal was not alone. Following right behind were three little babies. That made it even more interesting for me.

I came out from under the bench just to say *hello* and maybe make a new friend. Just then that *thing* decided I was coming too close to her and her babies. It turned right around in front of me, lifted up its tail and **Baboom, babaam** *a* thick, oily golden-brownish substance came *flying* right at my face and whiskers. I tried to protect myself by putting my right paw in front of my eyes. The mother skunk had sprayed me. She felt her babies were in danger and she was going to protect them. Mom could smell the stink inside and came running outside. But it was too late, the skunk had already done her damage.

I started salivating and rubbing my face on the ground to get rid of the stink. It did not work. ***"Mow, mow,"*** I cried out for help. Mom ran inside and grabbed some rubber gloves and an apron. Luckily, she was prepared for any kind of situation. She got out the skunk deodorizer and mixed the powder with water in a bucket. Oh no, first I get sprayed by a skunk and now I am going to be dunked into a bucket of water. I did not think that was fair!

Had I not been punished enough with that awful smelly spray that came from the skunk? Into the bucket I went. Mom was talking to me while washing me off over and over again. Then she wrapped me in a towel and dried me off.

"Eighty, I hope you learned a very important lesson today. First of all you did not listen when I had told you to *stay put*, and secondly never, ever mess with a Mother Skunk," Mom said. All I could do was *blink* at her with my green eyes in total agreement. She knew then that I had learned a valuable lesson.

24

It took several baths to eliminate the awful odor. Puppy and Oreo held their noses up high. They both had experienced an encounter with a skunk many years ago. One never forgets **that** kind of stink! They both felt sorry for me. Even though I was still a little stinky my two companions cuddled up next to me for the night.

Some time has passed since my family and I went on that exciting trip, and yet I am still a little **smelly**.

After everything that happened to me, my parents and friends still love me, and that is the most important thing.

And you know what? I am ready to go on another adventure at anytime.